With any level of higher education, what you learn and how well you learn it for that particular field can be made easier, if you understand the format in which it is taught, and thus learned.

Hopefully you are reading this for the first time, and have never taken California's world-famous baby bar, known officially as the First Year Law Student Examination.

The First Year Law Student Examination is exclusive to California, it was started back in the early 20 century according to some writings, and is also known as one of the most difficult examinations in the world. Other little known facts is that in terms of actual testing time, it is the longest test in America, and traditionally 8 out of 10 examinees fail.

I0510262

A. THOMAS ARCHIIR

I wrote this publication in the hopes of providing a thought process for you to succeed, and I share specifics that I have learned, that you must too, to give yourself the best opportunity to succeed, at the end of the day, that is really anyone can ask for.

Here, I will cover what I learned from a multitude of sources, and the reason why it is essential now more than ever to learn what used to be common protocol for exam takers, is now changing, and what you must do in order to have the very best chance at passing.

Before we get started, I wanted to take this opportunity to thank all of my Colleagues from Harvard, and all of my law professors from around the country, Jay, George, Steve, Mary, Aaron, Jeff, and Alan: Thank you!!!

Leadership excellence impact

A. THOMAS ARCHIIR

In order for you to be able to sit for the **First Year Law Student Examination**, also known as "The Baby Bar," you must have completed either through your work, or school the necessary requirements that create eligibility.

SOURCE: California Business and Professions Code

6060. To be certified to the Supreme Court for admission and a
license to practice law, a person who has not been admitted to practice law in a sister state, United States jurisdiction, possession, territory, or dependency or in a foreign country shall:

   (a) Be of the age of at least 18 years.
   (b) Be of good moral character.
   (c) Before beginning the study of law, have done either of the following:

(1) Completed at least two years of college work, which college work shall be not less than one-half of the collegiate work acceptable for a bachelor's degree granted upon the basis of a four-year period of study by a college or university approved by the examining committee.

(2) Have attained in apparent intellectual ability the equivalent of at least two years of college work by taking any examinations in subject matters and achieving the scores thereon as are prescribed by the examining committee.

NOTES:

This examination is known as the most difficult in the United States, and even many practicing lawyers today would have great difficulty in passing it.

It is also the longest exam in the country, it consists of a total test time of 7 hours broken down into 8 hours of writing in the morning, and three hours of multiple choice in the afternoon.

Check-in time is 7:30 A.M., then a break for lunch and a return time of 1:30, the bar exam ends at 5:30 that day.

It is given twice a year on a Tuesday, generally the last Tuesday of June and October.

Once you have completed this major task and are preparing for the exam, I suggest you pay for the exam on the first date of eligibility, and reserve your hotel now, and most times you do not have to pay until you show up at the hotel.

A. THOMAS ARCHIIR

5

This is important because the closer you get to the day of the exam, the room rates go up tremendously, if you can find a room at all.

By taking care of these two items, it will allow you to focus on what you need to do and provide two less items to worry about. Also in many jurisdictions the date you pay for the exam, decides where you will sit.

In fact some law schools require that their students all pay for their bar exams on the same day, thus allowing for classmates to sit with one-another throughout the entire examination.

Those that wait until the last minute, will be sitting with all of the other procrastinators, in the back of the room, with the entrance and exit noise a constant distraction.

Besides, if you are a procrastinator at heart, now is the time to stop that habit. Being a procrastinator in law can be quite expensive, especially when dealing with filing deadlines, and response due dates.

If this is you, break the habit now, get with your friends and pay together, study together when applicable, and clear this portion of the preparation from your to do list, then study with confidence. This is probably the only thing close to any control you may have for the exam.

Do not be an "undercover law student." This means that those you come in contact with, must understand what you are trying to achieve, you will get heartfelt words of encouragement, and stories about so-and-so who did finally pass. Most of all the people in your lives will understand, that what you are trying to achieve, is a Nobel act, reserved for the brightest minds in the world, yes that is you...

A. THOMAS ARCHIIR

One of my colleagues from law school shared a story about how he ran across a tutor, and was given a lot of study material, by someone who had just passed the exam.

He said that he had been looking to move closer to his job, and found a home that was perfect for him, In talking with the parties, he mentioned that he was in school, and would soon be taking the bar.

A young lady present then exclaimed that she had just passed the bar, and had been recently sworn-in. She went on to say that it was her aunt who tutored her, and then offered the same that she studied with, to my classmate.

This classmate passed the exam on the first try, and developed life long friendships with two other local attorneys.

Another thing I found helpful was to join your local bar, as a student member.

A. THOMAS ARCHIIR

The cost is around $30, and you get all of the benefits associated membership as an attorney. This includes, magazines, free webinars, and even social events reserved just for bar members.

I have met many great people this way, and I consider them to be friends, they also appear to be happy to discuss, and help me with the law, when I need understanding.

Let's Get Started!!!

The morning portion of the examination consists of 4 hours of writing in the morning, on 4 different and distinct sets-of-facts, these are called essays.

The subject matter tested is only 3 areas of law, criminal law, contracts, and tort law.

Contract law has two different areas that may be tested, one if the common law, and the other is the Uniform Commercial Code, UCC. This could technically make it four areas of law.

While the bar does not specify how a student should write about those subjects, most students who pass use the IRAC method of writing:

I.R.A.C. METHOD

Under, Here, Therefore are the simplest words to open each area of the IRAC sentence, examples below:

Issue = Can Tom win in his Suit against Bob? (This is the question the examiner wants you to answer.)

Rule of Law = Under Contract law the rule states

Analysis = Here, Tom will argue that because

Conclusion = Therefore Bob has the better legal position

These four items may sound simple, but what goes into writing them effectively for passing is really where the challenge lies...

A. THOMAS ARCHIIR

Issue

Generally speaking a way to determine what an issue and if it should be written about occurs when the student reads something in the essay that a rule of law can be applied to, it is that simple.

An example of issue spotting can be found it the following passage:

Carol a 6 year old wants to sue the grocer...

What should have come to your mind based on these facts is:

Guardian ad litem

Contract law

Tort law

Criminal law cannot apply here, and generally should not be discussed at great length, if at all.

Issue spotting is that easy, but you must know the law, in order to see and write about it.

NOTES:

Rule

The rule of law is multifaceted, but since the baby bar only tests on three subjects, you must choose from those three.

Many of us who have earned the privilege of taking this exam have backgrounds outside of law, it is essential that if those backgrounds are not that of a law student, then you must not discuss this "Superior Knowledge" in your exam answer.

If this happens, you may confuse your grader, besides it is probably well beyond the scope of what you must write about to pass this exam, remember you are being tested on what you learned in your first year of law school.

Do not bring in other subject matter that is not first year, contracts, criminal law, or torts,

A. THOMAS ARCHIIR

no matter how tempting, write about only subjects which are the basis of the exam.

Finding the appropriate law to write about is simple, because you are only being tested on three areas of law. The call of the question is what the author of the essay wants you to write about, this will also determine which of the three areas of law you will write.

For Criminal law, the call of the question will include, what charges can be brought. Again by process of elimination we know that charges only apply in first year law student exams in criminal law.

For Contract law, look for the call of the question to include rights or remedies available, then right on contract law.

Before writing on contract law, you must determine which contract law governs the facts in the essay, if is for the sale of goods,

A. THOMAS ARCHIIR

then the Uniform Commercial Code will be written about as the applicable law, if not then write about common law, and define it before you start writing using the IRAC method.

NOTES:

Analysis

When writing you analysis portion of the IRAC keep in mind that what you write is just as important as how you write, and most everyone agree, this is by-far the most important and difficult task you will face in the exam. For this reason, it is mandatory that you practice writing the elements you will be analyzing, I will cover that later in this publication.

When writing your analysis, you must first determine what roll you, the author, is playing. To complete this important task you must ascertain if you are being asked to be the prosecutor, the plaintiff, or the defendant. This is determined by the call of the question, meaning what is the author of the essay asking you to write about.

A. THOMAS ARCHIIR

Because the law is argued, this means there are two sides, one cannot argue alone, because it takes two-to-argue. In fact the words reasonable and appropriate depend on what side you are on.

As a writer in an essay, you must not only see both sides, but you must argue both sides, there is an appropriate way to open your analysis sentence, and when done properly, the other side argument will flow as a rebuttal.

Sometimes the essays will be so convoluted with facts and people that we have a tendency to avoid analyzing then in our writings.

The examiners know this and know that students who do not address these facts are not in compliance with what is required to receive a passing score.

A. THOMAS ARCHIIR

For this reason, do not ignore them, you must find a way to write about those convoluted facts, and try you best to make an argument that will support whoever you have decided has the stronger case.

This is essential and you should start practicing on this area of writing now, so that when you see it, you will be better prepared.

Res Ipsa Loquitor

When in doubt, use Res Ipsa Loquitor to define your answer.

Res Ipsa Loquitor means: That thing speaks for itself and can go a long way when dealing with convoluted circumstances on an essay.

By writing this, you will show the examiner that you have the confidence to let them know that what the essay states, does not make much sense, and that you understand that even in real life, that can be the case, Res Ipsa provides a great exit avenue and will allow you to move on to other areas of the essay, without ignoring vital key points of argument.

Objective Theory of Contracts

Where you have a contract case, the fall back for contract formation is: The Objective Theory of Contracts.

The Objective Theory of Contracts is also a fall back for convoluted contract issues where the parties have performed, it is defined as:

A principle in U.S. Law that the existence of a contract is determined by the legal significance of the external acts of a party to a purported agreement, rather than by the actual intent of the parties.(Farlex legal)
A. THOMAS ARCHIIR

First key words for writing an appropriate Analysis Paragraph

For Criminal law, write this as your analysis open: ***"Here the state will argue"*** this is because the state is the prosecutor, and they have the burden of proof, therefore in many jurisdictions the state goes first, but keep in mind, and only write this if the call of the questions asks you to be the voice of the prosecutor.

However, if you are asked to write as a defendant, then you would write "***Here the defendant will argue.***

In the immediate subsequent paragraph you would words indicating you are starting a counter argument, such as "However the state *(in rebuttal)* will argue, then compare the two arguments, and come up with an "likely"

A. THOMAS ARCHIIR

winner between your two arguments, based on where you are going with your essay, meaning the conclusion you want to reach.

It is important that you do not ignore facts, an example would be someone said the car was beige, and the defendant has a brown car.

The author of these words understands what everyone else does when they see the difference in the color of the car.

Most students would ignore these facts, because they have concluded that brown is not beige, but your failure to acknowledge the similarities as earth tone colors may cost you points, and failure to write on it, will show laziness on behalf of the examinee, this perception should be avoided.

A. THOMAS ARCHIIR

For contract law, or tort law, the opening of you analysis portion of the IRAC method must be, here *the plaintiff will argue, or here the defendant will argue.*

Identifying the actors in your writing

Historically most characters in an essay are named after the alphabet, you will see names like Abel, Betty, Carl, and Dave. (ABCD)

When writing an essay it is okay to use the first initial to define which actor you are referring, this is important, but can be confusing, so you must consider several factors when you decide to refer to the plaintiff as A, and the defendant as C.

Those factors are time, and the facts presented in the essay, if they are not convoluted, I prefer the Plaintiff or just the letter P, or the defendant of just the letter D, however when you have many plaintiffs or defendants, this style is not the best, for the reasons of distinct communication requirements on all legal writings.

Important key words to use when writing you analysis include: Moreover, and Additionally, this is one of the reasons while practicing sentences using those words will benefit you greatly.

So make time to just write using those words, or similar ones, while they may seem easy to use, they are not, especially under stressful situations.

Be careful not to over use those words, they are fancy and dominant, and overuse may dampen their intended impact, which is to sound and write like a lawyer. The proper use of those words go a long way in providing that impression to the grader.

A. THOMAS ARCHIIR

Remember there are two sides to every story, and you must tell both sides in order to win, but how you write is just as important as what you write. Please see my publication on mastering the basics; eliminate greatly, the guess work out of writing for the bar. In that publication you will see, and learn how to win at writing on negligence, homicide, contracts, and the Uniform Commercial Code.

One student recently told me he did not know these things until after he passed the exam, he passed because he scored an 85 on the multiple choice questions, making all of this stuff contained in this read, almost laughable.

A. THOMAS ARCHIIR

Conclusion

First of all when we discuss the conclusion, it is about the "C" in IRAC and nothing else, conclusionary writing is discussed in other publications of this author.

When writing your conclusion, you are being asked for a reasonable conclusion, based on which arguments you believe will win.

I always liked and learned to open the conclusion paragraph of the IRAC writing style with the word therefore. While others use different words to open, the word therefore has a ring of legality, and remember this is what the reader wants to see. When you are given an opportunity to use these words in your writing, take it.

Remember, unless the call of the questions specifically asks you; who is likely to win, or what will the trier of fact decide, you must avoid definite conclusions of winners or losers.

Your task on most essays at the conclusion portion of IRAC is to decide the likely outcome, and the reason why you feel this way. Do not write what the author did not ask you to write about, reach your conclusions in an open format, and write using these examples, unless told to do otherwise:

Therefore the plaintiff is likely to prevail, because when the D slapped her face, there was no consent or privilege mentioned in the facts.

Now on those same facts, another student could write his conclusion this way:

Therefore the defendant will win because when he slapped the plaintiff, it was part of a school play, and the plaintiff knew how to present her face for slapping, and did so, this clearly shows consent.

Now if the author of this exam, knew his facts did not include a conclusionary style in the latter example, you may lose valuable consideration required to pass, so be careful.

I was originally taught to keep my conclusions simple, and some professors like it that way, and others do not, ultimately it is up to you to decide how you conclude, but remember, as long as you have a conclusion, you have completed the IRAC style of legal writing.

A. THOMAS ARCHIIR

The majority of the time, you will be left with facts that are razor sharp and could go any way, so be careful, because no matter how you write your conclusion or decision on the winner or loser you must take into account the facts written in the essay.

If the author did not ask you for this, do not write on it. Some professors like a definite and precise conclusion, and some facts may call for this style of writing.

In a lot of essays, the facts do not specifically state who is a clear winner, or loser, this is why your analysis is so important, and the way you have discussed the law and facts, in the form of a legal argument, which must contain both sides to create the argument.

How you ultimately decide your legal conclusion as to who wins and who loses is not that important. When passing essays are published, they usually have one passing

A. THOMAS ARCHIIR

essay that has concluded for the opposition, and vice-versa.

I was originally taught to keep my conclusions simple, and some professors like it that way, and others do not.

Ultimately it is up to you to decide how you conclude, but remember, as long as you have a conclusion, you have completed the IRAC style of legal writing.

Do not leave law in your mind, put it on paper.

NOTES:

The importance of adding the "because" word in your writings.

When you are writing in law, you must tell the reader why some fact does or does not apply to a given element of the rule of law.

So is the rule of law has an element that states "the subject must be present," you then need to show the reader that the subject was in fact present at the time of the matter at issue.

Since the rule uses the word must, instead of shall, should, or could etc., the examinees written answer must clearly indicate the presence of the subject.

Example: Goliath must have been present because he caught the ball in the end zone and scored a touchdown, though no other facts other then these exist, presence can be

A. THOMAS ARCHIIR

inferred and if he was not present, he could have not scored the touchdown to win the game.

I am sure there are many better and more direct examples available for you to learn to use the word because in your writing.

It is this reason that you must look at the published essays and see how that key word is used in all of the legal writing that is successful.

NOTES:

Writing using the "plain text rule"

This fancy sounding legal term means that the writing contains nothing that can allow a statement to have two meanings or interpretations.

An example can be found in the 10 Commandments.

Thou shall not Kill.

This statement makes the reader understand without question what it is that the writer means.

To conquer this style of writing you must practice it, and when coupled with the words because, you are well on your way to writing a passing exam, and putting the hardest exam in America behind you…

Using the computer on your exam

If you are going to use a computer on the bar exam, it is essential that you familiarize yourself with the software before the date of the exam. This is very important because the features of underline, bold, and italicize should be used in your presentation to the grader of your work.

By learning how to work the software, you can easily go back to a previous exam, maybe to cut-and-paste, or to make sure you remembered to write a key point of the previous exams. Learn how it works now, familiarize yourself with all available functions, such as spell check, and auto-correct.

While in the middle of my exam, I recalled that earlier when writing on a Murder, on a previous essay, I suddenly remembered that I had failed to define Homicide. This omission could have failed my entire exam, but I knew how to get back to that essay, because I had practiced, and beat up the software while in the comfort of my own home. Thus I was able to go back to that earlier saved essay with confidence, and I added my definitions of Homicide, then moved, back the middle of my other essay.

Do not be afraid to call the manufacturer of the software and ask questions. I did, and the wait was not too long, and the representative seemed knowledgeable, patient, and willing to assist.

Important to note that when you are sitting in the exam, and the proctor tells the examinees to open the software, a new screen will appear that is slightly different from the one you studied.

A. THOMAS ARCHIIR

When this happened to me, it scared me beyond belief, because the screen prompt was requesting a password to enter the exam software. All of the passwords I tried failed, and because the "no talking warning: had been given by the proctor, I had no one to ask about this.

I started to really worry that I would have to hand write my exam, and my mind began to race, because I had not ever practiced handwriting any exam in law school before.

Thankfully and eventually the proctor announced to the examinees where the password for this examination could be found. It was on one of the pages in our exam hand-outs. So, in the event this happens on your exam, do not be like me, as you now will know that you are not alone, and where to find your password.

A. THOMAS ARCHIIR

In order to be accepted into the elite club of being a lawyer, you must comply with the rules in place, if you try to ad new ones, or fail to follow those in place, not one of them will let you in their club, so be sure to comply with club rules.

Working with words in parenthesis

Many times your essay will contain words that are in "parenthesis," e.g., " she kicked the rear door," in the event you see those words in yours, they must be included in your answer in order for you to pass the exam.

Example: The rear door got damaged by defendant *because* " she kicked the rear door," do not be afraid to cut-and-paste here to make sure the quote is correct.

This is an elite club member trick, and the graders are waiting to see if you too, are ready to become a member of the group.

Quality study time v. Quantity of study time

You MUST make time to STUDY, this means physically every hour available. The easiest way to do this is to study in a method or approach that will allow you to learn.

Some people are readers only, and do not, or, cannot listen to the lectures or definitions via audio publications, but instead must read them to understand, or are more comfortable just reading, or Vice-versa. Just like reading is important, audio is just as important, because the same way you learn to sing the words to your favorite song, can be applied to learning and recalling the law.

For others who audio provides their best learning environment, you must read, and learn how exam passers are formatting the passing essays, see every period, comma, and high-lighted areas. Remember, Success, breads success, and you must help yourself, at every opportunity, and learn what you must learn to pass, no exceptions!!!

With respect to the difficulties in understanding the law and issues which occurs sometimes, one of my favorite professors states; "you have no choice but to understand it."

So make sure when preparing that you find a way to understand what you are reading, because on the exam, you will be faced with far-fetched facts, with many actors, and laws, but by practicing the difficult readings now, you will have the mind set and confidence to remain competitive during the exam.
When practicing and taking the exam, do not leave the law or legal rules in your head, put it on paper. The following words should never be part of your legal academia, "I knew

A. THOMAS ARCHIIR

that." Do not assume the grader knows what you know. You must show them that you not only know that law or rule, but also how it applies to the facts in the essay.

On a recent exam, the facts had children who were intentionally and negligently injured, by a plaintiff.

On the call of the question, you were asked what legal rights and remedies the children had, they were 6, 7, and 8 years old.

After the exam was published, it hit the class rooms for discussion.

The professor had been provided both failing exams, and passing ones from students who had sat for that exam, he advised that the students had been given scores by the bar ranging from 55 to 80.

Many of the essays were about the same length in pages, but the passing answers, had more law, law that all of us know, but those that did not pass, apparently did not feel at the time of the examination those laws were appropriate, or important enough to write about.

One difference between the 60 answer and the essays scored above 70 was two well known and simple areas of law, that would have taken minutes to cover. They were guardian ad litem, and substantial factor test, also *the passing answers had smaller paragraphs, but essentially the same content...*

Making difficult interpretations

Some professors and the bar examiners like to use these foreign or weird names for the actors names in his essays. This used to drive me crazy, making me think "can't you just keep everything simple," after all you are naming the parties.

A. THOMAS ARCHIIR

While reading with comprehension necessary to understand the essay, I now have to worry about how to pronounce this name, or think of another name to give that actor.

What I have subsequently learned is that this is a very effective way to teach what you will probably face on the bar exam, and studying before hand will allow you to understand and thus react to the style of the author, and what is expected to be a passing answer.

The author of the exam knows the model answer, this is true for the bar graders too, so you just as well practice writing essays with the funny city, or weird actors names in them, and be better prepared for those weirdo's, when you see them on the bar exam.

While practicing, place yourself mentally in the exam at that time, keep an eye on your clock, then realize what you are missing, or what is lacking now in your knowledge. It is better to find that out now, remember it,

A. THOMAS ARCHIIR

correct it, and apply it.

The authors of the exam, have months, and years to write these exam questions, and you only have an hour to answer them, so be prepared to overcome this temptation, or lazy way out.

Understanding the **difference between the words, shall, must, could, may,** as they apply to legal writing, and understanding of the law is essential. So make sure you do know these differences when you read them in your essay, it could be the difference between a correct writing, and one not so correct.

This publication is for educational purposes only, and represents my experience, but remember this is your exam, and you must prepare using many sources of information, due to the ever-changing examination formats, and both the required and expected contents, that you exam answer must contain.

A. THOMAS ARCHIIR

Because of this I recommend using the many alternate methods of learning academic law as a good solid foundation, and remember this, learn-it-then-confirm-it, the law that is...

Please realize that the results of your exam, is in your hands, and preparation, repetitiveness, and legal logic MUST become a substantial factor if you are planning on passing your Bar Examination.

GOOD LUCK TO YOU !!!

BE SURE TO READ OTHER PUBLICATIONS BY THIS AUTHOR, THEY INCLUDE:

JULY 2014 Bar Exam "RETAKERS ESSENTIALS and SURVIVAL GUIDE"

13 MUST KNOW Principles for the Bar Exam

A. THOMAS ARCHIIR

www.ingramcontent.com/pod-product-compliance
Lightning Source LLC
Chambersburg PA
CBHW070717180526
45167CB00004B/1516